BITTERNESS

HENRY W. WRIGHT

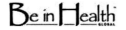

4178 Crest Highway
Thomaston, Georgia 30286

www.beinhealth.com

EAN: 9 781934 680117

Copyright Notice

Disclaimer

This ministry does not seek to be in conflict with any medical or psychiatric practices nor do we seek to be in conflict with any church and its religious doctrines, beliefs or practices. We are not a part of medicine or psychology, yet we work to make them more effective, rather than working against them. We believe many human problems are fundamentally spiritual with associated physiological and psychological manifestations. This information is intended for your general knowledge only. Information is presented only to give insight into disease, its problems and its possible solutions in the area of disease eradication and/or prevention. It is not a substitute for medical advice or treatment for specific medical conditions or disorders. You should seek prompt medical care for any specific health issues. Treatment modalities around your specific health issues are between you and your physician.

We are not responsible for a person's disease, nor are we responsible for his/her healing. All we can do is share what we see about a problem. We are not professionals; we are not healers. We are administering the Scriptures, and what they say about this subject, along with what the medical and scientific communities have also observed in line with this insight. There is no guarantee that any person will be healed or any disease be prevented. The fruits of this teaching will come forth out of the relationship between the person and God based on these insights given and applied. This ministry is patterned after the following scriptures: 2 Corinthians 5:18-20; 1 Corinthians 12; Ephesians 4; Mark 16:15-20.

Preface

This booklet was developed from a teaching to a live audience and has been kept in a conversational format. It is designed to reach a personal level with the reader rather than present a structured, theological presentation. Many times the reader will feel that Henry Wright is talking directly to him/her. The frequent use of the pronoun *you* is meant to penetrate the human heart for conviction, not for accusation.

TABLE OF CONTENTS

LOOKING DILIGENTLY
LEST ANY MAN
FAIL OF THE GRACE OF GOD;
LEST ANY ROOT OF BITTERNESS
SPRINGING UP TROUBLE YOU,
AND THEREBY MANY BE DEFILED.

HEBREWS 12:15

BITTERNESS

THE INVISIBLE KINGDOM

An understanding of the invisible, satanically ruled kingdom of evil spirits could be called Demonology 101.

Ephesians says,

> **Put on the whole armour of God, that ye may be able to stand against the wiles of the devil...**
> Ephesians 6:11

It is vitally important to understand there is a devil. Without this fundamental belief we make Jesus Christ a liar. He said, "I saw Satan fall like lightning from heaven."

> **And he said unto them, I beheld Satan as lightning fall from heaven.** Luke 10:18

Where did he fall to? Pluto, Saturn? Maybe even in the rocks of Mars? He fell into the second heaven. He was kicked out of the third heaven into the second heaven. The second heaven is between the first heaven and the third heaven.

Lucifer, the Archangel

Satan was kicked out of heaven because of rebellion. Not only for his own rebellion, but because he led others into rebellion as well. He led all of creation, including one-third of all angels into rebellion against God. He was kicked into the environs of the earth because that is where he was ruling in the world before Adam when he was Lucifer.

He was one of three archangels (Gabriel, Michael, and Lucifer) administering the government of God in creation in that old age. The Bible teaches he exalted himself above God. He said, "I will be like the most High God. I will exalt my throne above the clouds. I will exalt my throne above the stars, and I will exalt my throne above God's throne."

> **13For thou hast said in thine heart, I will ascend into heaven, I will exalt my throne above the stars of God: I will sit also upon the mount of the congregation, in the sides of the north:**
> **14I will ascend above the heights of the clouds; I will be like the most High.**   Isaiah 14:13-14

He tried it and encouraged others. He promised them a world without God. He promised them rulership; he promised them many things, and God judged them all.

Disembodied Satan

No one has ever seen Satan. He is disembodied in the second heavens; he is judged. Every invisible being that fell with him is disembodied; they are judged. They were stuck in a place the Bible refers to as the dry place.

It is a place of torment for the invisible beings because it is a place of non-existence, a place where they are trapped. They are not in heaven; they are not on the earth. They cannot do anything; they have no way of fulfilling themselves because there is nothing to fulfill.

They are tormented in the decadence of their own natures. The spirit of lust is tormented because it must manifest. Bitterness is tormented because it must manifest by its fallen nature. He must have the fulfillment. It is like any individual who is tormented by a breakdown in his nature, he is compelled to manifest that reality. There is a strategy, a stratagem, and a thought process that must be fulfilled.

Principalities

Satan's kingdom wanted access to Adam and Eve. The tree of the knowledge of good and evil was in the garden, because that was the test of Adam and Eve's obedience to God. God told them not to eat of the fruit of the tree because in the day they would eat of the fruit, they would surely die. It was a very simple test and they blew it.

Ephesians says,

> 10Finally, my brethren, be strong in the Lord, and in the power of his might.
> 11Put on the whole armour of God, that ye may be able to stand against the wiles of the devil.
> 12For we wrestle not against flesh and blood, but against principalities, against powers, against the rulers of the darkness of this world, against spiritual wickedness in high places.

13Wherefore take unto you the whole armour of God, that ye may be able to withstand in the evil day, and having done all, to stand.

Ephesians 6:10-13

We wrestle not against flesh and blood. What does that mean? We wrestle not against each other as humans. Someone may have a spiritual problem and you may be exposed to it, or they may be exposed to you.

If you are exposed to someone else's spiritual problem, the battle you are having with them is not with them as a person. It is with the principalities and powers, the invisible forces within them that have overtaken them and are acting out their nature through them.

This is who you are battling with. This is what this scripture is talking about. We wrestle not against each other, against flesh and blood, but against principalities; this is the bureaucracy of Satan's kingdom right here.

You have Satan. Then you have principalities. That word principalities comes from the Greek word *archeo*, which is also the root word for architect, or grand designer. Grand designer of what? The overthrow of God and God's kingdom in the earth.

We wrestle not against flesh and blood, but against

1) principalities

2) against powers,

3) against the rulers of the darkness of this world, and

4) against spiritual wickedness in high places.

Many of you may find these creatures living within your spiritual existence. You may identify with their nature in others or you may identify with their nature within yourself. However, if you are honest with yourself, today could be a day of deliverance for you. To know the truth can make you free.

> **And ye shall know the truth, and the truth shall make you free.** John 8:32

Now you have a decision to make whether you want to hang onto these things or you want them gone. If you do not fall out of agreement with these things, it is not God's fault, it is not my fault, it is not the guy-next-door's fault; it is your sin. That is why we need to repent and why we need to take responsibility.

Groupings and Hierarchy

Zoology is the identification of the animal kingdom by phyla and subphyla. The kingdom of principalities and powers answering to Satan, evil spirits that are invisible in the heavenlies and intruding into the lives of mankind, is structured just that way. There are groupings, there are legions, and there are clusterings of evil spirits.

When I see one spirit manifesting in a person, I know all the rest in the cluster are also in that person. If I see one of those critters raise its ugly head in someone's life, I immediately know there are anywhere from seven to seven hundred more right behind the scenes. I know all of them there by their nature. There is a graduated bureaucracy of Satan's kingdom in mankind from the upper echelon of principalities, down to powers, down to lesser entities. If I see a lesser entity, then the prince is still there. If I see the prince, everything under him is still there.

Discernment is by observation. If you want to pray for something, do not pray for the gift of miracles; do not pray for the gift of healings. Pray for the gift of discernment first, because without that we are all in trouble. Know your enemy and have your eyes wide open.

The church is so afraid of evil today and is so busy pretending evil does not exist that we are all victims. There seems to be this mentality in the church, out of sight, out of mind. Out of sight, out of mind is not a spiritual principle because Ephesians chapter 6 says we should be able to stand against the wiles of the devil. Another scripture says we are not ignorant of Satan's devices.

> **Lest Satan should get an advantage of us: for we are not ignorant of his devices.**
> 2 Corinthians 2:11

If you are not able to discern what is in the second heaven, which is the spirit world ruled by Satan, principalities, powers and evil spirits, you may be in trouble. You may be like someone driving down the road at night at 60 miles per hour with the headlights off. You may be going somewhere, but you may not have any discernment at all.

How do you discern? You watch someone's actions. You hear what comes out of their mouth. You see the fruit of their life. When you look, you will see which area is unrenewed; an area in which they are oppressed or possessed or controlled by the devil. The Word of God says that whatever is your master, you are its slave.

Can a Christian have an evil spirit? We could debate all day about whether a Christian can be possessed by an evil spirit; that is not the question. The question is this: does an evil spirit have a Christian?

You may say the evil spirit is not inside you, but he is in the tree next door projecting. The nature of Satan and his kingdom is involved in your life. It is obvious to me, it is obvious to God, it is obvious to many people around you and it should be obvious to you.

Is Satan Omnipresent?

We often use the term "the devil" as if it were Satan himself. Satan is not omnipresent, he is not omniscient; in fact, right now he could either be in this room or he could be somewhere else in the world. In Job 1, the Lord asked him, "Where have you been?" Satan replied: "I have been walking up and down throughout the earth."

> **And the LORD said unto Satan, Whence comest thou? Then Satan answered the LORD, and said, From going to and fro in the earth, and from walking up and down in it.** Job 1:7

Satan did that because he was administering his bureaucracy. He gave those that answer to him instruction as to what he wanted them to do to overthrow the government of God and bring mankind into captivity and separation from God on all levels. That is the grand design. It happens through direct abuse. It happens through direct evil, and it happens as insidiously as religion through ways of thinking, mindsets and perceptions. Satan will use anything he can to deceive because his name literally means the deceiver.

If Satan has deceived you, you are in deception. Ignorance is a form of knowledge. You may be ignorant and think you are smart. But if you are deceived, you will not know you are ignorant. People who are ignorant do not know they are ignorant. They think they are right.

Ignorance is a form of knowledge. There are many people that are sincere, but they are sincerely wrong. The only basis for truth and non-deception is the standard of what the Word of God says about any subject. Everything else is suspect.

There is a grouping of evil spirits that answer to a principality. Remember there are levels. An evil spirit may be a lesser entity, but he is answering to someone up the line that has more authority than he has. Ephesians 6 deals with principalities, powers, spiritual wickedness in high places, and the rulers of the darkness of this world.

The word "world" is the Greek word *cosmos*, translated as mankind. It's important to understand positionally where they are. Satan, through these evil spirits and this principality, can gradually bring you into captivity and control your life. Each spirit that answers to this principality is increasingly worse than the first one.

Remember the scripture says when an evil spirit is cast out, it wanders through a dry place looking for a place of rest, and finding none comes back to its original house to see if the house is filled or garnished and swept. Finding the house garnished and swept, it comes back into its original house and brings seven more much worse than itself and the latter state of that individual is worse than the former state.

> 24When the unclean spirit is gone out of a man, he walketh through dry places, seeking rest; and finding none, he saith, I will return unto my house whence I came out.
> 25And when he cometh, he findeth it swept and garnished.
> 26Then goeth he, and taketh to him seven other spirits more wicked than himself; and they enter in, and dwell there: and the last state of that man is worse than the first. Luke 11:24-26

What does it mean to be filled up or garnished?

If I cast an evil spirit out of you, yet you were not filled up with the knowledge of God and you were not filled up with the antidote to what that thinking and that part of your nature represented, you would be just a vegetable. You would be just blank in that area of your life. But I fill you up with knowledge about a subject.

That is why we teach and teach, and teach, and teach. Probably the worst thing I could do to you is to just deliver you and send you home. If you do not have a foundation to stand on from the Word of God and you are not filled up with the knowledge of God, then you do not even know what you have been delivered from. Then you are easy pickings. Every evil spirit that has been cast out of you, at some point in your life, will come back to check you out to see if you are home or out to lunch.

When my enemy comes back to me in areas of my life God has delivered me from and comes knocking on my door, I am not out to lunch. I am wide awake and I know what is going on here. I have the Word of God.

When that spirit comes knocking on my door in an area of temptation or a feeling or a thought or an idea progressively to lead me down the highway of captivity again, I back off and say, "Get behind me Satan. I know you. I have been there, I have done it, I am not going there again." I know what I have been delivered from. I want to get rid of everything that is not of God. I want every bit of my stinking nature to be changed.

It is not your kingdom anyway; it is His kingdom. You have been created for God's pleasure. The question is this: are you giving God pleasure? Each of these spirits is progressively more dangerous than the other, more powerful than the other and when the final spirit interacts, the conclusion of the matter will literally produce spiritual and physical death.

What is woven with holiness in your ability to be there on that day in the resurrection and see the Lord? Following peace with all men.

> **Follow peace with all men, and holiness,**
> **without which no man shall see the Lord:**
> Hebrews 12:14

If your lifestyle is to slander, stir up, cause trouble, speak evil, gossip and carry on, then your soul is in jeopardy. Your very salvation is in jeopardy and if you do not think so, go to Revelation chapter 2 and 3 and read what the Lord has to say to five of those seven New Testament churches.

There are those who teach eternal security, but that is a heresy. I believe in eternal security as long as you stay eternally secure in God through Christ Jesus; but if you think God is going to let you run amok as an evil reprobate in this earth, you can forget it. If you are not sure, read Ezekiel chapter 18. Read Revelation chapters 2 and 3 concerning what the Lord Himself had to say about the church.

> **Looking diligently lest any man fail of the grace of God; lest any root of bitterness springing up trouble you, and thereby many be defiled;**
> Hebrews 12:15

What does it mean to fail of the grace of God?

Galatians says if any man is overtaken in a fault, or a spiritual defect, those who consider themselves spiritual, restore such an one in a spirit of meekness and consider yourself also, lest you be found in the same spiritual defect and fall away.

> **Brethren, if a man be overtaken in a fault, ye which are spiritual, restore such an one in the spirit of meekness; considering thyself, lest thou also be tempted.**   Galatians 6:1

Paul, in Romans 1, said what you accuse another of, you are yourself. What you accuse another of while excusing yourself from the same spiritual problem, you have the same problem.

When I find people saying, "Well, I want to tell you something about Tom..." Do you know what? The thing they are saying he has, they have.

The very same thing they are pointing out as a fault or a failure in another person, they themselves have the same spirit within them. It is a smoke screen. They think, "I get over here, I make sure Tom knows he has this problem, but now I will be safe, because I am well hidden, I have good discernment." Paul said, "Baloney! You have the problem."

If brother Tom has a problem in his life and if you are so spiritual you discern it in him, don't go over to Don and say, "I have to talk to you about Tom, man. He has a spiritual defect. You need to know about it." You should come over to Tom and say, "Brother, I am spiritual, I want to help you, I want to love on you, man; I want to get close to your heart, I want to meet you, man. I want to bear up under you. Could I come along beside you? Can I represent the Lord to you?" That is a spiritual man.

God is spiritual and He is so righteous and so spiritual He could knock every one of you dead in your tracks because of your sin right now and have every right to do so. He is spiritual; your Father is spiritual; Jesus is a spiritual man. They have come with grace and mercy and said, "OK, reprobate, I love you man." That is a spiritual man.

THE KINGDOM OF BITTERNESS

This kingdom of Bitterness will separate you from God and damn your soul. Understanding this phylum of evil spirits and principalities we are exploring will prevent that from happening.

If you find any one of these evil spirits in your life, every single one can damn your soul. I do not care whether you say you are saved or not, it can damn your soul if you do not come to grips with it. You are worth saving.

An open rebuke is better than secret love and I love you. The hardest thing for me to do is to tell people the truth. I would rather take a whipping than have to stand before you and confront you on the things that will damn your soul and carry you into apostasy, bondage, disease, insanity and into desolation. Every single one of you is worth saving.

Hebrews 12 says this: Looking diligently lest any man fail of the grace of God, lest any root of Bitterness spring up within you and cause trouble. Then who is defiled? Many are defiled.

Have you been around anyone who has the root of Bitterness? Do you know what Bitterness looks like in a person? Have you been exposed to Bitterness in your life? Does it take much discernment to see it?

No, you did not have good discernment because you looked at the person who was bitter and you copped an attitude towards them because you thought they were the devil. They are not the evil spirit. There is an evil spirit in them that makes them that way and they are the victim. You are so spiritual you believe they are the enemy and so you take them on for size and Bitterness comes up in you.

Now we have a game called Bitterness ping-pong. Your Bitterness against my Bitterness. When you are in Bitterness ping-pong, everybody is defiled.

Bitterness and His Armor

Hebrews 12:15 says, Strong man is my name. Bitterness is my game.

Luke 11 says, I trust in my armor.

Ephesians 6 says, Our battle is not with flesh and blood, but against principalities and powers, spiritual wickedness in high places.

The Bible says unless you bind the strong man, you cannot spoil his house. He is very smart because he is a principality. He knows how to get you because he has gotten many just like you for hundreds and hundreds of years and he is very skillful.

Luke says,

> **20But if I with the finger of God cast out devils, no doubt the kingdom of God is come upon you.**
> **21When a strong man armed keepeth his palace, his goods are in peace:**
> **22But when a stronger than he shall come upon him, and overcome him, he taketh from him all his armour wherein he trusted, and divideth his spoils.**

> ²³**He that is not with me is against me: and he that gathereth not with me scattereth.** Luke 11:20-23

You are the palace he wants to live in. He is in the second heaven and he is tormented. The Bible says when an evil spirit is cast out, it wanders through a dry place seeking a place of rest. When he is not in someone as a spirit, he is not at rest. When the evil spirit is in someone, the evil spirit is at rest and the person is at unrest; but when the evil spirit is cast out, the person is at rest and the evil spirit is back at unrest.

He wants to be in your house. You are his palace. If he gets in there, then Jesus said in Luke chapter 11 he is going to strut around upstairs, walk in your kitchen and your living room, sleep in your bed, and he is going to put you down in the basement in a prison house. He is going to walk around in your body and you are going to be deep inside wanting out, but you cannot do anything about it because you let him in to begin with.

There is only One who can get him out and that is someone stronger. Who is stronger? Jesus. Who is stronger? The Father. Who is stronger? The Holy Ghost. Do you know who else is stronger? Someone coming along anointed with the Holy Ghost in the name of the Lord Jesus to cast him out. In Mark it says believers shall cast out devils.

> **And these signs shall follow them that believe; In my name shall they cast out devils; they shall speak with new tongues;** Mark 16:17

Jesus said in Luke 11 when the evil spirit is in his place of abode in you, he is the strong man and he is very content his armor is going to keep him in a place of superiority in your life. He is the prince of Bitterness, he

...itect, but he has some workers going after ... they want you, too.

Unforgiveness

Let's say someone has one of these workers already in them. It could have been your mother or your father, your brother or your sister. It could have been anyone who had this problem from the beginning.

Hebrews says Bitterness defiles many others. So all of a sudden here you are at 12 years old and you are exposed to someone else's Bitterness. The principality in this person wants to get you too, and will do or say anything to make you a victim.

Something has been done to you and there is a spirit on assignment immediately in conjunction with the spirit operating in the other person. What is the first thing that comes into you when someone wrongs you? Unforgiveness.

Bitterness is the strong man and the first piece of armor he trusts in is Unforgiveness. He is banking on the fact that once Unforgiveness is part of your life, you are never going to forgive and he is going to have his place and his habitation.

What Bitterness is banking on is you remembering a record of wrongs. He is banking on the spirit of Unforgiveness reminding you of Bitterness someone has against you. The task of Unforgiveness is to remind you, rehash it, bring it up, project it, and torment you with it.

Unforgiveness is like instant replay. Unforgiveness will replay the words, the voices, the sights, and the sounds. Unforgiveness will flash at you everything others ever said. That is a spirit playing a recorder over and over again to reinforce itself so the strong man of Bitterness can stay.

Resentment

After Unforgiveness has had its fermenting work in your life, then the strong man sends out another spirit to reinforce the first one that now has a foothold in your life. That spirit is called Resentment. Resentment stands on the foundation of Unforgiveness. The record of wrongs is now fermenting. A spirit of Resentment fuels the fermentation of Unforgiveness.

Resentment defiles you by saying: "You know what? I really don't like you. I resent you. I'm never going to forgive you. I am bitter against you. I resent you."

Because you are feeding off the foundation, you are now the armor. Unforgiveness is the armor. Bitterness is trusting the spirit of Unforgiveness will stay in you. He is trusting that now Resentment will get a foothold so he can get a chance to be the king of the palace in your life.

You can have two people with the spirit of Bitterness and both will play back against each other to reinforce it. One can resent the other. This is how the other one responds: "Hey, you think you can resent me? You ain't seen nothing from me yet." So you have the reinforcement of it back and forth because there is more than one principality of Bitterness, there are tens and hundreds of thousands of strong men running around wanting access to people's lives.

There is a whole kingdom, millions of invisible entities, that wants to control you and they want access to you at this level so they can fulfill their nature. Here you have an interplay going on because you picked up the fact of Resentment.

You can see how it can accentuate and accelerate and how the defilement can become complete. This is what we call the beginnings of a permanent breach. As one responds to the other we have a sparring match going on.

All of a sudden the strong man is going, "Yes, I knew it would work!" If you are not careful, there will be a spirit in someone else that will interact with the spirit in you. Both of you are now victims, and you do not even know it.

Many times Unforgiveness is an intellectual thought because it is in the memory. Resentment is there like the fuel to the fire. You feel Resentment right in your belly.

You think it in your head. You are thinking in your memes and your memory, but an evil spirit lives within your human spirit. Your human spirit is in your abdomen and that is why you feel it right in the empty cavity because that is where your spirit man is.

> **He that believeth on me, as the scripture hath said, out of his belly shall flow rivers of living water.** John 7:38

That is where the Holy Spirit lives within that spirit dimension of your existence. You are a spirit, you have a soul and you live in a body.

Retaliation

After Unforgiveness and Resentment have gained their foothold, the next spirit the strong man sends out to be armor for himself is Retaliation. Once Unforgiveness and Resentment have become part of your life, it is time to get even. Retaliation.

"I'm going to get even."

I remember a bumper sticker I saw a few years ago, "I don't forgive, I just get even."

"You're going to pay; I remember what you did to me."

"These feelings are real, you're going to pay."

"You better watch your back, I'm going to get you if it is the last thing I ever do."

This spirit of Retaliation is much more dangerous than Unforgiveness and much more dangerous than Resentment. The latter state of a person who has Retaliation is worse than the person who just has simple Unforgiveness. It is progressive hierarchy. Each spirit is much more dangerous.

This reality probably accounts for 99% of mankind's problems. In ministry if I see someone who wants to get even and the person says, "Well, they are going to pay," instantly I know a spirit of Resentment is in there, a spirit of Unforgiveness is in there, and the strong man of Bitterness is behind it all. I know somewhere there is a record of wrongs. When you see any of these spirits that are up the line, they are all there.

If I am going after a spirit of Retaliation in ministry, I am going to be after a spirit of Unforgiveness and the spirit of Resentment also. The higher we go on the order of evil hierarchy, every one of this armor is there reinforcing the one just above it.

What is reinforcing Retaliation? Resentment. What is fueling Resentment? Unforgiveness. What is the root of it all? Bitterness. There is an entire kingdom of evil spirits, each one by its own major nature. I have been in ministry for many years, and I have seen them all.

I have heard them say, "Well, you might have gotten Unforgiveness, but I'm Retaliation and you're not going to get me. I'm going to get even anyway. You might have cast out Unforgiveness, but I'm not going." The spirits have argued with us, they have fussed with us and they have debated with us.

Anger and Wrath

When Retaliation has established itself within you, there is another spirit Bitterness sends out to reinforce the other three. That is Anger and Wrath.

Unforgiveness can be hidden. Resentment can be hidden skillfully by someone who is deceptive. Retaliation can be hidden, but Anger starts to show physically.

Have you experienced Anger and Wrath because of your root of Bitterness, because of your Unforgiveness, because of your Resentment, because of your Retaliation? Has anyone ever gone to this level of Anger and Wrath in your life? You know when the buttons are pushed, and that strong man of Bitterness is getting his foothold, this is the armor he is trusting in.

Anger and Wrath never occur unless these three, Unforgiveness, Resentment and Retaliation have been festering for some time. You get angry for a reason. The reason is because of the breach, because of the hurt, because of the victimization, Unforgiveness, Resentment and Retaliation got their foothold. Now we have the fourth spirit that comes.

Let's go back and understand something. This is a fermentation stage for a physiological open statement against another. Retaliation is internalized long before the act of getting even. When you see all seven of these spirits manifest, you are going to understand how it can progressively become part of your nature.

Yes, Retaliation may seem worse than Anger, but this is the fermenting stage. The final conclusion of Bitterness is Murder. The final act of Retaliation is Murder, either physically or murdering them with your tongue. You are going to eliminate them.

Retaliation sets the stage to eliminate, but you will not eliminate anyone unless you have Anger and Wrath working within the spiritual dynamics of this principality and the spirits that create and answer to it.

We are dealing with Anger coming out of relationship. This is the Anger and Wrath tied to

Bitterness. This is a progression of spiritual dynamics producing the elimination of a person in relationship.

It is the root behind all people who murdered someone and are in prison. It is the root behind all family splits, behind all division, and behind all breakup of human relationships. This is the kind of Anger and Wrath we are talking about.

The Bible says to "be angry and sin not." There is an anger not tied to this type of thing. However, this Anger is part of a progression producing a final breakup in human relationship permanently.

We are trying to unravel the progression of each of these spiritual dynamics that is much worse than the former, producing a final fruit the Bible talks about. If you from your heart do not forgive your brother his trespasses, which produces the Bitterness, your Father which is in heaven cannot or will not forgive you yours.

We have to eliminate this strong man in order to be free. Luke 11 says when the strong man is armed he keeps his palace, his goods are in peace and when one stronger than he comes upon him, then he shall take from him all the armor in which he trusts and divide the spoils.

> 21When a strong man armed keepeth his palace, his goods are in peace:
> 22But when a stronger than he shall come upon him, and overcome him, he taketh from him all his armour wherein he trusted, and divideth his spoils. Luke 11:21-22

Resolution

In order to defeat the strong man, you have to understand his armor. You have to understand what is in front of him that is involved in your life that you have to deal with so he can be dealt with and you can be free. The fruit of all this is your peace with that person, if at all possible. If it is not possible, you still can be free and be freed by God whether there is any resolution with that person who created the breach or not.

You do not have to have resolution with a person who has injured you in order for you to be free because the resolution comes from God. If you say, "I will give up Bitterness when I have resolution with the person who hurt me," then you are in idolatry to that person. Resolution of these things in your life does not depend on resolution with that person.

However, God would want you to have a heart towards resolution with that person. If people do not respond because they have a root of Bitterness, because they are into Retaliation, Resentment, Unforgiveness, and Anger and Strife, then that is not your problem. You have to come before God personally and get your freedom.

The strong man is banking on the fact that Unforgiveness will act as a flash card forever to allow the Retaliation, Resentment, Unforgiveness, and Anger and Wrath to continue to work in you. Your healing and your freedom depend on all roots of Bitterness being dealt with in your life.

Unforgiveness is a Fruit

Unforgiveness is a fruit of Bitterness. If that was not true, then Hebrews 12:15 would have said "looking diligently lest a root of Unforgiveness springing up trouble you." You must be able to forgive. Bitterness comes before Unforgiveness every single time. Bitterness is the root. Unforgiveness is the fruit of the root.

You must be able to forgive your brother his trespass from your heart. It is the condition of your freedom. If you do not forgive your brother his trespass, his Bitterness and his roots of Bitterness which have defiled you in all categories, then you have set yourself in a place where God cannot forgive you of your trespass. That is a high price to pay.

God forgives all manner of sin. If you are sons of God, you must be able to forgive as your Father in heaven forgives. Because you have a new nature, you forgive. Bitterness is defeated by one stronger than himself and that is what God has done through Jesus Christ. You have the opportunity to fulfill that in your life.

Hatred

After Anger and Wrath has gained their foothold, Hatred comes. Hatred now not only has the root of Bitterness, but it is being fueled by Unforgiveness, Resentment, Retaliation, and Anger and Wrath. Now begins the stage of elimination.

Hatred says this: "I exist on this planet and you do too, and one of us has to go and it will not be me. I hate you, I can't stand you. I hate you, I resent you, I am going to get even and you do not belong on this planet."

Hatred involves the elimination of the other person. Retaliation was the fermenting stage of this. Anger started to vocalize it and now Hatred comes to help execute it.

This is the fuel for the progression of a final victimization by your enemy. When you see Hatred in a person, you know that Anger is there, Retaliation is there, Resentment is there, Unforgiveness is there, and Bitterness is there and he is trusting in his armor.

Bitterness is banking on the fact when you are ready to forgive, old Unforgiveness will pull up a flash card of voices, sights and sounds and smells reminding you of what they did to you.

If that is not enough, Resentment says, "Now, let me help you really feel it right here."

You really feel it, don't you?

"But I am trying to forgive them." "No, you really resent it."

Retaliation then says, "Yeah, besides you didn't get even, did you? They need to pay."

Then Anger says, "Yeah, and I am going to go tell them just what I think, and if I do not tell them, I will tell someone else."

Then Hatred says, "Yeah, I am not only going to get even, I am not only going to retaliate, but I am going to cause them some damage. I hate them."

Violence

You can see Violence in everyday life in families. This is the progression of breakup of human relationship out of Bitterness. Bitterness is behind all domestic Violence and all juvenile Violence.

This is what puts people in jail and this is why we have a police force, because this sixth level of Bitterness is Violence. Violence is Anger and Hatred in motion, because it is not just emotional anymore, it is not just spiritual, it has now become physical.

The voice of Violence sounds like this: "You know I hate you so much, I am just going to punch your lights out. I am going to punch your lights out. I am going to tear you apart. I am going to tear your house apart. I am going to do some physical damage."

In relationship breakdowns at this level, I have seen pots and pans get thrown across the room. I have seen teapots get thrown across the room. I have seen scratch fights and cat fights. I have seen wrestling matches.

I have seen everything in domestic violence and abuse you can think of in parents and children. This is physical abuse. Women are capable of it too, not just men. I have seen women physically abuse a husband. It is not just a man always abusing a woman. I have seen it the other way.

Bitterness is banking on the fact that this progression in your life is going to keep him in place, and these spirits are able to generate their nature in you and also in others to fuel this thing back and forth.

Murder

The seventh spirit that completes the full plan of the devil for destruction out of this strong man of Bitterness from Hebrews 12:15 is the final one. It is the spirit of Murder.

The spirit of Murder is not just physical murder; in the Word it says murder with the tongue. Murder can be found in the heart, because the conclusion of the spirit of Bitterness is the elimination of the person on all levels. It is the breach that is the problem.

The world is filled with Murder. It is filled with anarchy, division, sedition, Violence, and it is filled with Bitterness. It is in the world; it is in the church; it is in our families; it is in our nation; and it is in our personal lives. Do you know why?

You cannot have a family without people. You cannot have a nation without people. You cannot have a church without people. You are the target of this strong man Jesus was talking about in Luke 11, if he gets into your heart and he sets up his throne within your life, he is the strong man, he is armed, and he keeps his palace.

SANCTIFICATION

It is amazing how much you powder your nose, brush your teeth, put on perfume, buy pretty clothes, but these Bitterness characters are a stench. You ought to be as concerned about these as you are your toothpaste. The most tragic thing is to see a beautiful person in the natural have a very ugly spirit.

Listen to what the Word says about the woman: it is not her jewelry she wears, it is not the clothes she buys at Saks Fifth Avenue, but what makes a beautiful woman in the eyes of God is a meek and quiet spirit.

> ³Whose adorning let it not be that outward *adorning* of plaiting the hair, and of wearing of gold, or of putting on of apparel;
> ⁴But *let it be* the hidden man of the heart, in that which is not corruptible, *even the ornament* of a meek and quiet spirit, which is in the sight of God of great price.   1 Peter 3:3-4

A meek and quiet spirit is of great, great beauty to God. You can be meek and quiet and it does not mean you have to be a wimp. The Bible says Moses was the meekest of all men. He had a little Fear and he had to get his brother to speak for him, but when it came to obeying God, he listened to God.

The number one scripture you ought to have next to John 3:16 is in Mark.

> ²⁵And when ye stand praying, forgive, if ye have ought against any: that your Father also which is in heaven may forgive you your trespasses.

> 26But if ye do not forgive, neither will your
> Father which is in heaven forgive your
> trespasses.   Mark 11:25-26

John 3:16 is that GOD so loved you, the world, that He gave His one and only begotten Son. I said, His one and only begotten Son. He so loved the world.

> For God so loved the world, that he gave his
> only begotten Son, that whosoever believeth in
> him should not perish, but have everlasting life.
>   John 3:16

Hebrews says to follow peace with all men.

> 14Follow peace with all men, and holiness,
> without which no man shall see the Lord:
> 15Looking diligently lest any man fail of the
> grace of God; lest any root of bitterness springing
> up trouble you, and thereby many be defiled;
> 16Lest there be any fornicator, or profane
> person, as Esau, who for one morsel of meat sold
> his birthright.
> 17For ye know how that afterward, when he
> would have inherited the blessing, he was
> rejected: for he found no place of repentance,
> though he sought it carefully with tears.
>   Hebrews 12:14-17

The writer instructs his readers to follow peace with all men, and holiness. Many people struggle with holiness. "Well, I do not measure up to God. You know God is perfect and I am not perfect, and oh well, so what, forget it." Well, do not go there. Isaiah said holiness is a highway that is traveled.

> And an highway shall be there, and a way, and
> it shall be called The way of holiness; the unclean
> shall not pass over it; but it shall be for those: the
> wayfaring men, though fools, shall not err therein.
>   Isaiah 35:8

What did Isaiah mean when he said holiness is a highway that is traveled? Holiness is a progressive movement in a certain direction, by which your nature is transformed from Satan's nature into God's nature.

That is righteousness. You are being changed. The way you think, the way you speak, the way you act is being changed into the image of the living God because that is what you lost in the fall. You lost the nature of God.

God said in Genesis 1:26, "Let's create man in our image." What is the image? God's nature. Not just His nature, but the very definitions of the soul, the spirit and the body. God has a spirit body. He does not have a physical body in the understanding as we know of physical things.

However, we lost God's nature because of sin. That is why we needed to get born again. That is why our spirit needed to come alive to God because our nature had died to God.

Our spirit was dead to God, but now our spirit needs to come alive to God because who we are spiritually is who we really are. That is the person God wants to see in heaven. He does not want to see a corrupt, individual in heaven.

Hebrews 12:14 says, "Follow peace with all men and holiness without which no man shall see the Lord." So what is going to separate you from your salvation and your seeing the Lord one day? Number one, not following peace with all men; number two, not desiring holiness. Those two areas are very, very critical.

THE INGREDIENTS TO PERFECTION

What is perfection as far as God is concerned?

In the Bible it talks about what God has said by the Spirit of God about certain elements of your thinking and your spiritual reality and if you applied these things to your life, the Word says you shall never fail. How would you like to walk through life and never fail?

Before you can have a more excellent way and walk in your life without failing, these characters of Bitterness have to be dealt with. They will engineer circumstances through other people and yourself to keep you from your peace.

It is impossible to follow peace with all men if these characters are in your life. It is impossible for someone else to walk in peace with you if these characters are in their life.

These things will separate you from God and from His peace. They will separate you from your own peace, and they will separate you from peace with other people. That is why they have to go.

Looking Diligently

> **Looking diligently lest any man fail of the grace of God; lest any root of bitterness springing up trouble you, and thereby many be defiled;**
> Hebrews 12:15

Notice this scripture goes both ways. You may be exposed to another person's Bitterness, or you may be the perpetuator of Bitterness against yourself. You have

31

to look at this two-way mirror. Do not point the finger at someone else because you have three more coming right back at yourself. Look at it both ways and allow yourself to judge yourself. The Word says if you judge yourself, God will not have to judge you.

You have an opportunity to start looking deep into your own spirit, to see if any of these characters are part of your life. You have the ability before God and God's provision and His anointing and His Word. If you are sincere, He can deliver you of these things. If you go through the methodology like a religious road, you can forget it.

Jesus said,

> **So likewise shall my heavenly Father do also unto you, if ye from your hearts forgive not every one his brother their trespasses.** Matthew 18:35

You say, "Well, they have not repented to me." It does not make a bit of difference. It is not what they do; it is what you do.

If you are exposed to someone operating in any one of these areas of Bitterness, they have failed in the grace of God and what are you going to do about it? What if you fail in these areas and you have the Unforgiveness, Resentment, Retaliation, Anger, Hatred, Violence, Murder, and the Bitterness?

When you subject another person to that you have failed in the grace of God. You have fallen short of the glory of God. The glory of God is His nature, which is perfect in all its ways. The earth shall be filled with the knowledge of God; the earth shall be filled with the glory of God.

> **For the earth shall be filled with the knowledge of the glory of the LORD, as the waters cover the sea.** Habakkuk 2:14

Does that mean it is just a bright, shining light going around we are blinded by? No, the glory of God is His nature. The holiness is His nature; righteousness is His nature. God is perfect in His relationship and He is not going to compromise it for any reason. He will meet you in it.

Paul said,

> **Brethren, if a man be overtaken in a fault, ye which are spiritual, restore such an one in the spirit of meekness; considering thyself, lest thou also be tempted.** Galatians 6:1

If you are "overtaken in a fault," it means you have a spiritual defect. You have fallen short of the glory of God. Paul tells you how to deal with it. If a brother be overtaken in a fault, those of you who consider yourself spiritual, restore such a one in a spirit of meekness.

It does not mean we retaliate back and forth. It means to restore such a one in the spirit of meekness and consider yourself also lest ye be tempted in like manner and fall away.

Remember this is a two-way mirror. You cannot point the finger at anyone. You are going to have to look both ways. There are two dimensions I want you to consider. The first dimension is what others have done to you. The other dimension is what you have done to others. Part of your freedom will be to forgive others, but the second part is that you be willing to get rid of it yourself because you have done it to others.

Conviction

I am not going to let the devil come here now in condemnation. Some of you are going into great conviction and some into condemnation. Conviction is of God; condemnation is of the devil.

Conviction is of God and if your hearts are convicted, then respond to conviction. If your hearts are condemned, it is the devil accusing you and we are not going to let him do that.

I want you to say with me,

> **There is therefore now no condemnation to them which are in Christ Jesus, who walk not after the flesh, but after the Spirit.** Romans 8:1

If you have this problem and you are submitting your life to God, you are starting to do something called "walking by the Spirit of God." If you allow something to rule your life and you are not interested in dealing with it, then condemnation comes.

If God comes and convicts you in an area of your personal life, what you need to do is to tell the devil of condemnation to shut up and look to heaven and say, "God thank you for showing this to my heart." God does not condemn you, the devil does. God is not condemning you because this is the dispensation of grace and mercy. God is not angry at you. You need to settle that in your heart.

You have to make your peace with God in this area. God loves you and He has accepted you through Jesus. He wants this evil gone out of your life, because it separates you from His love and it separates you from your peace, and it separates you from other people.

Continuing in Hebrews,

> **16Lest there be any fornicator, or profane person, as Esau, who for one morsel of meat sold his birthright.**
> **17For ye know how that afterward, when he would have inherited the blessing, he was rejected: for he found no place of repentance, though he sought it carefully with tears.**
> Hebrews 12:16-17

I want to give you a warning. It is a serious thing to take your spiritual freedom for granted. To willingly, wantonly and deliberately choose evil leaves you in a very precarious place. You are wide open for the executor of the curse to come into your life.

In the case of Esau, he did not respect his birthright. What was his birthright? His position of spiritual provision. You have a provision from God for peace. You have a provision from God for freedom from Fear. You have a provision from God for peace of relationship with God, yourself, and others. You have to be jealous for that in your life.

The Word says,

> **For where your treasure is, there will your heart be also.** Matthew 6:21

Is your treasure in peace or is your treasure in Bitterness? Do you want to live a life of peace or do you want to have chaos every single day of your life? I will tell you I enjoy peace of mind; I enjoy my birthright.

There is a warning right here in conjunction with the scriptures on Bitterness. We need to guard our hearts as to what is important in our life. You need to be zealously jealous for your own safety, and it is available to you from God.

Matthew 18

Matthew says,

> ¹⁵Moreover if thy brother shall trespass against thee, go and tell him his fault between thee and him alone: if he shall hear thee, thou hast gained thy brother.
> ¹⁶But if he will not hear thee, then take with thee one or two more, that in the mouth of two or three witnesses every word may be established.
> ¹⁷And if he shall neglect to hear them, tell it unto the church: but if he neglect to hear the church, let him be unto thee as an heathen man and a publican.   Matthew 18:15-17

If this scripture were executed by church leadership, we would have fewer problems. When you have someone who has offended you, do you go to them personally and privately to regain your fellowship and friendship with them? No. You find someone else first to listen to you and you take up the case with someone who was not even part of the ordeal to begin with.

What you are looking for is someone to take your side, agree with you without the facts, and then make a decision with no facts so you can load the gun with factless accusations. The end of it is you do not want peace with your brother anyway.

This is a battle to the death. You can go from Bitterness, to Unforgiveness, to Murder in your heart in no time.

If someone has offended you, go to them privately, alone. Get your peace and if they will not receive you, and they do not want peace, go get two or three more to go with you to bring peace, not in accusation, but as peacemakers. If it cannot be resolved, bring it to the church and they will hold court.

If the person still will not walk in peace, there can be no fellowship. Now, I do not execute these scriptures as quickly as they are written. I will tell you this: I am not afraid of it either. Bitterness and Hatred are killers. It is Murder in the first degree.

Binding and Loosing

This next scripture is usually quoted out of context and I want to set the record straight.

> [18]Verily I say unto you, Whatsoever ye shall bind on earth shall be bound in heaven: and whatsoever ye shall loose on earth shall be loosed in heaven.
> [19]Again I say unto you, That if two of you shall agree on earth as touching any thing that they shall ask, it shall be done for them of my Father which is in heaven.
> [20]For where two or three are gathered together in my name, there am I in the midst of them.
>
> Matthew 18:18-20

The context of these scriptures has to do with forgiveness. It has to do with the releasing of God's power for provision and protection because of forgiveness, or the releasing of Bitterness for destruction.

It has nothing to do with prosperity; it has nothing to do with healing. It has to do with the release of the kingdom of God, or the kingdom of Satan, in the hearts of men in the earth. You will find the question Peter asked, "How oft shall my brother sin against me and I forgive him?"

The entire context of these scriptures has to do with binding or loosing. Binding evil to your heart and evil to your brother's heart, or loosing the spirit of supplication, mercy and grace in the earth. It is your decision. That is why God hates Bitterness. That is why He will not forgive you if you do not forgive your brother because it violates the binding and loosing of love and forgiveness in the earth.

If you want to get on with God, you need to loose forgiveness and love into the earth. If you do not, you are binding yourself and mankind and everyone around you to Bitterness and Hatred in the earth and they shall rule.

You need to guard your tongues. You need to encourage everyone operating in this dimension to guard his or her tongue. If you agree with them and you do not follow the Scriptures, you are not only binding them to the curse, you are binding yourself to the curse.

All you gain is for the armor of Bitterness to become stronger and stronger in your life. It is no one's fault but your own.

That is why it said in the previous scriptures, if your brother offends you, go to him privately and tell him.

"We are not right together man, what is going on?"

"You ticked me off, I am not interested in talking about it."

"But Tom, I love you man!"

"Yeah, but you do not know what you did to me, you old goof ball. Get out of my house."

"OK, sorry man."

I go find two or three brothers to come knocking at Tom's door.

"I love you man, we have to resolve this."

"Get out of here!"

Next comes pastor.

"Tom, I didn't see you in church service on Sunday. You didn't receive your brother. You didn't receive him once to make peace, what is the problem? Either come and deal with it or we can't have fellowship with you."

If that were executed, a lot of people would make quick decisions for God. If I do not deal with you according to knowledge, then I am going to lose you anyway.

There are people trying to bind together in churches who have Bitterness and Hatred against each other and they wonder why the Spirit of God is not moving in the church. The Spirit of God is grieved at our hypocrisies; the Spirit of God is grieved at us not taking responsibility for love.

God came and died for you because of love. He was brutally massacred because of love. He took pain and grief and sorrow even to death because of love so the Scriptures might be fulfilled. "No greater love is there than a man who would lay his life down for another."

There is nothing more important in life than peace with God and peace with each other. Measured out in holiness of life, there is no greater honor and no greater place of spirituality.

Some of you will look in this door of the perfect law of liberty and you will peek in and you will like it. Then you will shut the door and you will walk back into your darkness. Some of you will walk through the door and this will be defeated forever. Your choice.

Unless this is dealt with at some level, your healing will not come because God is not going to give you a healing and let you keep Bitterness. It violates His very nature.

Why should He give you grace and mercy when you will not give anyone else grace and mercy? Why should He love you when you do not love others? Why should He give you a birthright you do not want?

Why should God free you of Bitterness? It is going to come right back in anyway if you do not operate according to the principles.

Let's go back to Matthew again.

> **18Verily I say unto you, Whatsoever ye shall bind on earth shall be bound in heaven: and whatsoever ye shall loose on earth shall be loosed in heaven.**
> **19Again I say unto you, That if two of you shall agree on earth as touching any thing that they shall ask, it shall be done for them of my Father which is in heaven.**
> **20For where two or three are gathered together in my name, there am I in the midst of them.**
> Matthew 18:18-20

If you bind Bitterness in the earth, it is bound in heaven. Whatsoever you loose in the earth shall be loosed in heaven. If you loose forgiveness into the earth, it is loosed in heaven. "Again I say unto you that if any two of you shall agree on earth as touching any thing that they shall ask, it shall be done for them of my

Father which is in heaven. Where two or three are gathered together in my name, there am I also."

Seventy Times Seven

Peter asked, "Lord how often shall I forgive my brother, till seven times? Jesus said, "No, seventy times seven."

> [21]Then came Peter to him, and said, Lord, how oft shall my brother sin against me, and I forgive him? till seven times?
> [22]Jesus saith unto him, I say not unto thee, Until seven times: but, Until seventy times seven.
> Matthew 18:21-22

Seven times seven is 49. Seventy times seven is 490. To help you understand the significance of what Jesus was saying, I have brought it to numerical understanding.

I break down my day into three sections: eight hours for work, eight hours for family and the Lord, and eight hours for sleeping. If you took an eight hour section of time, multiplied it times 60 minutes to the hour, you would have a number equaling 8 times 60, which is 480 minutes. 490 times exceeds that.

Jesus' answer to Peter in the normal arena of the day, with yourself, with others, in the work place, and with your family, if they sin against you in that same area every single minute of the day, minute by minute, release them and forgive them.

Every single minute of your day, in the same area forgive them and release them. Forgive them and release them.

If you do not forgive them and release them moment by moment, minute by minute, then guess who has a chance to come in and start occupying your mind? The strong man of Bitterness and the first spirit he sends on assignment to remind you of that breach is Unforgiveness.

You have to forgive. You have to separate the person from their sin, just as God separated you from your sin and forgave you. He forgave you and accepted you and you did not have it all together with Him.

He still accepts you and still forgives you every single minute of the day. "If we confess our sins He is faithful and just to forgive us our sins and to cleanse us from all unrighteousness." Repent.

Parable of the Ten Thousand Talents

Continuing in Matthew,

> ²³Therefore is the kingdom of heaven likened unto a certain king, which would take account of his servants.
> ²⁴And when he had begun to reckon, one was brought unto him, which owed him ten thousand talents.
> ²⁵But forasmuch as he had not to pay, his lord commanded him to be sold, and his wife, and children, and all that he had, and payment to be made.   Matthew 18:23-25

Ten thousand talents computed is worth about $19,200,000 dollars in today's money. There was a servant who owed his boss, $19,200,000.

"For as much as he had not to pay, his lord commanded him to be sold, and his wife and his children." A man who has a wife and a family can bring a curse on his family and his wife because of Bitterness.

I have seen families destroyed; wives and children pay a price because of a man's Bitterness. I have seen it cause so much trouble in the work place, the city, and the church, his family is just scorched with shame. There is a high price to pay.

His lord commanded him to be sold, his wife and children and all he had and payments to be made. Matthew says,

> ²⁶The servant therefore fell down, and worshipped him, saying, Lord, have patience with me, and I will pay thee all.
> ²⁷Then the lord of that servant was moved with compassion, and loosed him, and forgave him the debt. Matthew 18:26-27

That same servant went out and found one of his fellow servants, which owed him 100 pence, which is about $17. He laid hands on him and took him by the throat. This is the same servant who had just been forgiven $19,200,000.

> ²⁸But the same servant went out, and found one of his fellowservants, which owed him an hundred pence: and he laid hands on him, and took him by the throat, saying, Pay me that thou owest.
> ²⁹And his fellowservant fell down at his feet, and besought him, saying, Have patience with me, and I will pay thee all.
> ³⁰And he would not: but went and cast him into prison, till he should pay the debt.

> ³¹So when his fellowservants saw what was done, they were very sorry, and came and told unto their lord all that was done.
>
> ³²Then his lord, after that he had called him, said unto him, O thou wicked servant, I forgave thee all that debt, because thou desiredst me:
>
> ³³Shouldest not thou also have had compassion on thy fellowservant, even as I had pity on thee?
>
> ³⁴And his lord was wroth, and delivered him to the tormentors, till he should pay all that was due unto him.
>
> ³⁵So likewise shall my heavenly Father do also unto you, if ye from your hearts forgive not every one his brother their trespasses.   Matthew 18:28-35

You are asking God to forgive you of your debt. He already has through Jesus Christ. So what are you to do? Forgive your brother his trespass.

If, on the one hand you are asking God to forgive you, but on the other hand you will not forgive your brother, then Torment comes.

Where you have Bitterness, you have Torment. Where you have Unforgiveness, you have Torment. Where you have Resentment, you have Torment. Where you have Retaliation, you have Torment. Where you have Anger and Wrath, you have Torment. Where you have Hatred, you have Torment. Where you have Violence, you have Torment, and where you have Murder either with tongue or with deed, you have Torment.

If these are in place, it opens the door for Rejection. Rejection and all it represents opens the door to Fear, and Fear represents another deeper bondage. Whether it is Bitterness, Rejection, or Fear, all three of these areas are torment to your life.

If you have forgiven someone, you do not have to worry about Rejection. If you have forgiven someone, you do not have to worry about Fear. These have to go and never come back.

The Evil Spirit Seeks Rest

These spirits will try to come back. You can be set free of all of these spirits and five seconds from now you can be exposed to a person operating in these spiritual dynamics and you have a choice to make. You can choose to be a spiritual person and walk in your freedom, or you can choose to open the door for the spirit to come back into your life again.

That is why the Bible says the evil spirit comes back to its original house to see if the house is filled or empty.

> **43When the unclean spirit is gone out of a man, he walketh through dry places, seeking rest, and findeth none.**
> **44Then he saith, I will return into my house from whence I came out; and when he is come, he findeth it empty, swept, and garnished.**
>
> Matthew 12:43-44

What you are learning now, needs to be the foundational teaching for every believer from the first day they accept Christ. This is the first thing that has to get unraveled. If this is not dealt with in your life, all the other things you want to deal with will be that much more difficult to deal with.

This is holding the record of wrongs; this is doing the flashback; this is playing the old video camera; this is Accusation. This is what gets you into trouble with others.

This is what makes you hear voices in your head; this is what gets you into a place of Jealousy and Envy. This is what strategizes to separate you from God and others. That is why these spirits are so dangerous.

Forgive Our Debts

The Lord's prayer says,

> [9]After this manner therefore pray ye: Our Father which art in heaven, Hallowed be thy name.
> [10]Thy kingdom come. Thy will be done in earth, as it is in heaven.
> [11]Give us this day our daily bread.
> [12]And forgive us our debts, as we forgive our debtors.   Matthew 6:9-12

I tried to find the word trespass in this passage a few years ago and could not find it. We quote the Lord's prayer as forgive us our trespasses, as we forgive those who trespass against us. I could not find that in Scripture anywhere.

The original manuscript of the Majority Text is translated into debt and debtors. The reason for this is in conjunction with the parable in Matthew 18 about the debt we are owed and the debtors when we are in debt to someone. This has to do with forgiveness. Forgive us our debts as we forgive our debtors.

What does that mean? It means we forgive. We release others from their debt as they release us from our debt. Debt puts you in bondage to another.

When someone has Unforgiveness against you and you have Unforgiveness against them, then you have a breach. It is just as if it were a debt. It is unresolved until it is cleared. It stands right there demanding to be fulfilled as any debt would be.

If you want to be a free man or a free woman, then you need to be free with each other. That is why the Bible says if you loan anyone money and he or she cannot pay you, release them because that is a breach.

I remember a few years ago I ran a business selling construction supplies. There was a young man who was a trim carpenter and he bought a trim gun, an air gun and some supplies from me. I think the bill was four or five hundred dollars and this boy always had a problem paying his bills.

It went on 30, 60, 90 days and he still had not paid me a cent. We were attending the same church at the time. He came up to me one time and said, "I am just having a hard time on the job and I just cannot pay you." I said, "That is fine brother."

Well after 30, 60, 90 days I found when I came to church that I would see him and he would see me and then he would run down an aisle somewhere to avoid me. For the next month he avoided me. He was a precious brother; he just had some problems.

He owed me five or six hundred dollars, but he would avoid me. What was happening? There was a breach. I finally engineered a way I could intercept him and I did. I intercepted him and boy was he scared. You could see it all over his face.

I walked up to him and I said, "Listen, brother, there are two things I want to tell you. First of all, you have been avoiding me over the debt you owe me. But I want you to know something, you are more important to me than five or six hundred dollars. My fellowship with you is more important to me than five or six hundred dollars.

I am here to look you straight in your face and tell you I release you from the debt. You do not owe me anything. I want your fellowship more than I want the money."

He started to cry and said, "Are you serious?"

I said, "Yes sir, I am as serious as I can be. If you ever pay me, fine. If you never pay me, fine. I want my fellowship with you and you are worth more than five or six hundred dollars to Jesus and me. So I release you from your debt."

"The next time you see me, I want you to come, let's get our hug together, let's get our handshake, let's get our fellowship going, and then I'll pray for you that God will bless you in your business and do whatever it takes to bless you."

I never got paid, but he never avoided me either. That was only $500-600. I do not know what I would have done if it had been $19,200,000.

God is a restorer of the broken heart. God is the repairer of the breach. God is the one who will repair the desolation of many generations. This is the first day of the rest of your life, and in Christ, in the Father through Jesus Christ, whether you live or whether you die, you are the Lord's. Eternal life and resurrection from the dead is your promise.

Hebrews says if you fall away, there is no place of repentance for you again because you have crucified Christ all over again.

> **If they shall fall away, to renew them again unto repentance; seeing they crucify to themselves the Son of God afresh, and put him to an open shame.** Hebrews 6:6

God's grace and mercy in my life supplanted that scripture because I fell away in my hurt, in my rejection, stumbling over man and family members who rejected me, brutally assaulted me, and emotionally abused me. I found God loved me more than the judgment of His Word. He said, "I shall have mercy on whom I shall have mercy." Your debt might be only $19,200,000. My debt would have broken Fort Knox.

A Man's Enemies

Zechariah says about Jesus and that day in the Millennium when His throne is in Jerusalem and the nations are coming up to bow their knees before Him and worship Him as King of kings and Lord of lords, they see the scars in His hands. Zechariah sees prophetically into the future; they see the scars in the hands of Jesus Christ in Jerusalem.

They say, "Sir," because they do not know Him. They are Islamic, Buddhist, whoever they are from across the face of the earth. They have not been taught the ways of the Lord. They are just finding out who God is, who the Lord is, who the Father is and who redeemed saints are.

Kings and priests and the people are required to come up once a year, Zechariah says, to worship the Lord. They look at the Lord Jesus standing there in His place in Jerusalem, and they ask this question to the Lord Jesus: "Sir, where did you get these wounds?" His answer shall be in that day: "These are the wounds I received in the house of my friends."

> **And one shall say unto him, What are these wounds in thine hands? Then he shall answer, Those with which I was wounded in the house of my friends.** Zechariah 13:6

As Jesus was dying on the cross, His words are recorded: "Father, forgive them, they know not what they do." I pray that in this spiritual assault against your enemy you will have it in your heart to say, Father forgive them, for they know not what they do.

Matthew says,

> **¹²And forgive us our debts, as we forgive our debtors. And lead us not into temptation, but deliver us from evil:**
> **¹³For thine is the kingdom, and the power, and the glory, for ever. Amen.** Matthew 6:12-13

All of this is in the context of forgiveness. For if you forgive men their debts, your heavenly Father will also forgive you. But if you do not forgive men their debts, neither will your Father forgive you your debts. That is a high price to pay.

**When you ask God to forgive you
and you do not forgive another,
you are making yourself
greater than the living God**

He is greater than you and He forgives all sin. You, as a created being are lesser than Him in creation. If you do not forgive sin, you are in opposition to His heart.

God said,

> Be ye therefore perfect, even as your Father which is in heaven is perfect.   Matthew 5:48

Galatians says,

> [19]Now the works of the flesh are manifest, which are these; Adultery, fornication, uncleanness, lasciviousness,
> [20]Idolatry, witchcraft, hatred, variance, emulations, wrath, strife, seditions, heresies,
> [21]Envyings, murders, drunkenness, revellings, and such like: of the which I tell you before, as I have also told you in time past, that they which do such things shall not inherit the kingdom of God.   Galatians 5:19-21

Many people struggle over this because they see these things in their lives. Those who habitually practice such things without any conviction whatsoever, because of hardness of heart and the way of life, your salvation is in jeopardy. You are in the very same position as Esau who sold his birthright for a bowl of pottage.

Separation from God is a very high price to pay for Bitterness. Almost word-for-word, there is Hatred, Anger, Wrath, Murder. Sedition is coming out of Retaliation and Hatred. Those that practice such things shall not inherit the kingdom of God.

If you are struggling with Rejection and Fear of Rejection, Fear of Man, Fear of Failure, and Guilt, they are going to be almost impossible to dislodge in your life if we do not deal with Bitterness because this is the superglue that drags you right here.

Cain's Anger

Genesis says,

> ¹And Adam knew Eve his wife; and she conceived, and bare Cain, and said, I have gotten a man from the LORD.
> ²And she again bare his brother Abel. And Abel was a keeper of sheep, but Cain was a tiller of the ground.
> ³And in process of time it came to pass, that Cain brought of the fruit of the ground an offering unto the LORD.
> ⁴And Abel, he also brought of the firstlings of his flock and of the fat thereof. And the LORD had respect unto Abel and to his offering:
> ⁵But unto Cain and to his offering he had not respect. And Cain was very wroth, and his countenance fell. Genesis 4:1-5

Many people have debated for years why God made the distinction. It seems to be Cain just brought it out of requirement but Abel found something that was the best he had. Abel brought of the firstlings of his flock and the fat thereof. He went out and found something special for the LORD.

Cain felt rejected by God. Bitterness came in. Unforgiveness came in. Cain turned his Wrath against Abel and not against God. That is Jealousy and Envy. Cain was wroth and his countenance fell. That is Anger. He went from Bitterness to Unforgiveness to Resentment to Retaliation to Anger in his heart in no time.

The LORD said unto Cain, "Why are you angry? Why are you wroth and why is your countenance fallen down?"

A person who is very angry and very bitter looks the part. It did not take God much discernment to notice that. Discernment sometimes is not difficult. You just open your eyes and perceive.

What did God say? He didn't say, I perceive in my heart you are very bitter and angry. He says, "Why is your countenance fallen?" Why the pouty lip? Why the long face? Got a problem, son?

> **6And the LORD said unto Cain, Why art thou wroth? and why is thy countenance fallen?**
> **7If thou doest well, shalt thou not be accepted? and if thou doest not well, sin lieth at the door. And unto thee shall be his desire, and thou shalt rule over him.** Genesis 4:6-7

God said, "If you do well, you shall be accepted." In other words, in this case what I did in the offering with Abel and you, if you do well you shall be accepted, and if you do not do well then sin lieth at the door. Unto thee shall be his desire and you shall rule over him. Is that talking about Cain over Abel? It seems to be.

Cain talked with Abel his brother, and it came to pass when they were in the field Cain rose up against Abel his brother and did what? What is the conclusion of Bitterness? Murder.

The LORD said unto Cain, "Where is Abel thy brother?"

Cain said, "I know not, am I my brother's keeper?" Well, he lied, didn't he?

God said, "What hast thou done? The voice of thy brother's blood crieth unto me from the ground."

> [8]And Cain talked with Abel his brother: and it came to pass, when they were in the field, that Cain rose up against Abel his brother, and slew him.
> [9]And the LORD said unto Cain, Where is Abel thy brother? And he said, I know not: Am I my brother's keeper?
> [10]And he said, What hast thou done? the voice of thy brother's blood crieth unto me from the ground.   Genesis 4:8-10

When you do not forgive another and you have Bitterness against another and if you murder someone, even with your tongue, that stands as a screaming reality in the ears and face of God until it is resolved. The Bible says, "Every word that you have spoken shall be held against you in the day of judgment."

You talk about a massive video camera and massive recorders that have been playing over mankind for 6,000 years. In the Day of Judgment, God is going to look at certain people and say, "Did you say this or not? Did you do this or not? Did you forgive or not?"

"Well, yes I did."

"Peter, push the button," and here comes your voice.

"Is that you or not?"

"Yes God, that is me, I said that."

"Then why did you lie to me?"

Well, for the very same reason Cain lied to God – out of Fear. The only way out of it is in First John.

> **If we confess our sins, he is faithful and just to forgive us our sins, and to cleanse us from all unrighteousness.**　1 John 1:9

You tell someone, "I wish you were dead." What is that? Retaliation skipping right to Murder. Have you ever told anyone you wished they were dead in your Anger? Have you had anyone ever tell you in their Anger they wished you were dead? Have you ever told anyone to go to hell? Do you know what hell is? The grave.

You wish they were dead. When you do not take responsibility for your words for a curse against a person's life, "I wish you were dead," "Go to hell," whatever you want to say; if that is not dealt with before God, then the devil takes it and demands it be executed first against your life and then against the other.

When you come before God and take the responsibility out of a pure heart, out of conviction, and you ask God to forgive you, He will, and those words will not stand against you in judgment in that day. The other person is also released from that curse because you turn the curse into a blessing.

Much of our disease and destruction, people who are accident prone, people who are having terrible times in business, and people having terrible times in success of life, may have been cursed by someone in Bitterness. We need to take all the curses that apply to you and get them under the covering of God and His Word against the penalty and get the curse broken.

Your grandfather or your father may have stolen from someone, or moved a landmark, or may have ripped someone off in a business dealing. For a long time, I wished I could go back and talk to my daddy and find out what he had to deal with in generational curses.

I do not have to ask my father, I do not have to ask my grandfather, I do not have to ask my great-grandfather what their spiritual problems were. I know the areas of my life that were right there in my face.

I could go back to my father now and I could read his mail. I could tell him things about himself and he would blush, because I could read his mail. I could tell him everything about his past. I could even tell him about his grandpa. I know what us Wrights had to deal with.

The things you are struggling with probably have been in your family tree for generations. It can be broken and you can be released from that flowing of familiar spirits that want to duplicate themselves in your life generation to generation. We do not have to be victims anymore.

Your Brother's Keeper

Look at verse 10, "The voice of thy brother's blood crieth unto me from the ground." The object of your Bitterness is the destruction of your brother and the justice required on his behalf has come before me. You, Cain, are the responsible man. You yielded and now you are responsible.

> [11]And now art thou cursed from the earth, which hath opened her mouth to receive thy brother's blood from thy hand;
> 12When thou tillest the ground, it shall not henceforth yield unto thee her strength; a fugitive and a vagabond shalt thou be in the earth.   Genesis 4:11-12

The same curse you curse another with, you yourself are cursed with.

If it were not for Jesus and what He did at the cross for you, you are stuck with the deal. But the good news is, because of God's love for you and the provision He made for you from the foundation of the world, you can be set free from the penalty of this curse in your life and other people's lives.

You can be set free and the penalty can be paid because of what Christ did for you, and you can be released. But you are going to have to take responsibility. I wonder what would have happened if Cain had said to the Lord, "Yes sir, I am guilty, I am sorry, it was that strong man Bitterness. It was the devil who made me do it, God, and I yielded to the devil and I am sorry I killed my brother. I need deliverance." But did he say that? He said this, "Am I my brother's keeper?"

The Word of God says you are your brother's keeper! I personally as a human being, as a son of God, and as your brother in the Lord, have a responsibility before God to care for your heart.

"If a brother be overtaken in a fault, those of you who consider yourselves spiritual restore each other in a spirit of meekness." I have a responsibility to love you and to care for you and never to injure you and if I do, I take responsibility for it and repent.

We are human, we make mistakes, we have some of these characters that are still there. Rather than hiding from it and pretending and say, "No, I didn't say that," say "Yes, I did." I have some of those characters and one of them manifested; it was Jealousy of you.

That was not me, and I am spiritual and I can see it, it was not me! I do not think that way about you! Will you forgive me? Will you help me get rid of this thing? Do you see it in me too?"

"Yes, I do."

"Do you still love me?"

"Oh, man do I love you. I am able to separate you from that every day."

Because of Jesus' blood, forgiveness is possible. If we breach over misunderstandings, or a devil comes, then the blood of Jesus makes it possible to get our repentance and get our healing and get our fellowship restored so we can continue to walk in the light as He is in the light.

If we would practice this in our families, our churches and our lives, we would not have any wars, divorces, anarchy, Bitterness, and we would have a life of peace. But it is not possible without Jesus; it is not possible without the Father. Because the strong man armed keepeth his goods that his palace is secure in the earth until one stronger than he comes upon him and takes away from him the armor in which he trusts and spoils his goods.

Strife

Proverbs says,

> ¹⁵**The way of a fool is right in his own eyes: but he that hearkeneth unto counsel is wise.**
> ¹⁶**A fool's wrath is presently known: but a prudent man covereth shame.**   Proverbs 12:15-16

> ¹¹**The mouth of a righteous man is a well of life: but violence covereth the mouth of the wicked.**
> ¹²**Hatred stirreth up strifes: but love covereth all sins.**   Proverbs 10:11-12

Hatred is the root for Strife. When you see Strife going on between people, Hatred is the root behind it. But where does that come from? All the way back to the strong man. The Bible says where there is Strife, there is every evil thing.

Strife is the fruit of Hatred, and Hatred is part of the armor of Bitterness, and the strong principality of Bitterness is banking on the spirit of Hatred to stir up Strife. It is a matter of life or death. Hatred stirreth up Strife, but love covereth all sins.

John says,

> There is no fear in love; but perfect love casteth out fear: because fear hath torment. He that feareth is not made perfect in love. 1 John 4:18

Peter says,

> And above all things have fervent charity among yourselves: for charity shall cover the multitude of sins.   1 Peter 4:8

There is a scripture that seems to indicate one day in the future with God's people, because they have such hearts to repent, that when they sin He does not even pay attention to it. He knows them well and they are so on top of it, that when they trip in that breach of their spirit, in their thinking because they are human, they are so quick to discern it and so quick to repent and get it dealt with, He just continues on in fellowship with them because He knows their heart.

Ezekiel says,

> Thus saith the Lord GOD; Because the Philistines have dealt by revenge, and have taken vengeance with a despiteful heart, to destroy it for the old hatred;   Ezekiel 25:15

The Philistines were moved by old Hatred. Old Hatred is Unforgiveness and Bitterness. It is something that has been kept going year after year after year after year. It causes them to act despitefully and antagonistically against the Jews because they have dealt by revenge- Retaliation, Resentment, old Hatred producing war against God's people, which is rooted in Bitterness to produce destruction.

In Ezekiel this is a prophecy against Edom that was against God's people.

> Because thou hast had a perpetual Hatred, and hast shed the blood of the children of Israel by the force of the sword in the time of their calamity, in the time that their iniquity had an end: Ezekiel 35:5

Perpetual Hatred drove the people of Edom to murder God's people, the Jews. What is fueling this perpetual Hatred? Anger and Wrath. What is fueling it? Retaliation. What is fueling it? Resentment. What is fueling it? Unforgiveness. What is fueling it? Bitterness, perpetual Bitterness. A strong man in the nation of Edom, a strong man in the nation of Philistia to produce war, Strife, Murder, and Violence.

Death Rules

John says,

> 8He that committeth sin is of the devil; for the devil sinneth from the beginning. For this purpose the Son of God was manifested, that he might destroy the works of the devil.
> 9Whosoever is born of God doth not commit sin; for his seed remaineth in him: and he cannot sin, because he is born of God.
> 10In this the children of God are manifest, and the children of the devil: whosoever doeth not righteousness is not of God, neither he that loveth not his brother.
> 11For this is the message that ye heard from the beginning, that we should love one another.
> 12Not as Cain, who was of that wicked one, and slew his brother. And wherefore slew he him? Because his own works were evil, and his brother's righteous.

> [13]Marvel not, my brethren, if the world hate
> you.
> [14]We know that we have passed from death
> unto life, because we love the brethren. He that
> loveth not his brother abideth in death.
> 1 John 3:8-14

Now you know why we have so many problems
with disease. He that loveth not his brother abideth in
death. Rage and Anger, Bitterness, and Hatred are
responsible for a good 50% of all diseases that are
incurable and result in death. This is dangerous to your
health.

The spirit of Death is right here because Murder is
ruled by the spirit of Death. The spirit of Death, what
you do unto another, shall come back unto you. Even in
your heart as you meditate on the fruit of the nature of
this, it shall come back to you.

The blessings you bless with, you are blessed with.
The cursings you curse with, you are cursed with. It is a
simple and basic axiom. That is why the Bible says to do
unto others as you would have them do unto you.

Forgive, if you want to be forgiven. Give life if you
want life given to you.

> [14]We know that we have passed from death
> unto life, because we love the brethren. He that
> loveth not his brother abideth in death.
> [15]Whosoever hateth his brother is a Murderer:
> and ye know that no Murderer hath eternal life
> abiding in him.   1 John 3:14-15

This is not a physical Murder, but murdering
someone with your tongue and in your heart. Your
eternal security and your salvation are in jeopardy.

Remember Cain. Remember Esau, who sold his birthright for a bowl of pottage.

> Hereby perceive we the love of God, because he laid down his life for us: and we ought to lay down our lives for the brethren.   1 John 3:16

The Sin Within

Romans says,

> [28]And even as they did not like to retain God in their knowledge, God gave them over to a reprobate mind, to do those things which are not convenient;
> [29]Being filled with all unrighteousness, fornication, wickedness, covetousness, maliciousness; full of envy, murder, debate, deceit, malignity; whisperers,
> [30]Backbiters, haters of God, despiteful, proud, boasters, inventors of evil things, disobedient to parents, Without understanding, covenantbreakers, without natural affection, implacable, unmerciful:
> Romans 1:28-31

Hebrews says,

> Looking diligently lest any man fail of the grace of God; lest any root of bitterness springing up trouble you, and thereby many be defiled;
> Hebrews 12:15

Defilement comes from within your human spirit. From within your reality, out of your mouth, out of your action, out of your person, or someone else's person. This character and all those who answer to him operate to produce the murder and the death to the situation.

In Mark we read the words of Jesus concerning the thoughts and intents of the human heart.

> ²⁰And he said, That which cometh out of the man, that defileth the man.
> ²¹For from within, out of the heart of men, proceed evil thoughts, adulteries, fornications, murders,
> ²²Thefts, covetousness, wickedness, deceit, lasciviousness, an evil eye, blasphemy, pride, foolishness:
> ²³All these evil things come from within, and defile the man.   Mark 7:20-23

All these evil things come from within and defile the man. Murder is more than just physical death.

First John says if you hate your brother in your heart you are a murderer.

Romans 7 gives us the story of Paul and his personal spiritual life. I appreciate Paul's honesty in Romans 7. His battles and my battles are very similar. Perhaps you can identify with your battles.

Paul said,

> ¹⁵For that which I do I allow not: for what I would, that do I not; but what I hate, that do I.
> ¹⁶If then I do that which I would not, I consent unto the law that it is good.
> ¹⁷Now then it is no more I that do it, but sin that dwelleth in me.
> ¹⁸For I know that in me (that is, in my flesh,) dwelleth no good thing: for to will is present with me; but how to perform that which is good I find not.
> ¹⁹For the good that I would I do not: but the evil which I would not, that I do.

> ²⁰Now if I do that I would not, it is no more I
> that do it, but sin that dwelleth in me.
> Romans 7:15-20

Paul says twice that the evil he hates to do as a man of God, he does. He also repeats twice that it is not even him doing it, but it is sin that dwelleth in him, operating through him, that is doing this. He, by participating with it, consents unto the word that the Word is wrong, and the new law coming that he is abiding by is true and that would make the Word of God error.

> ²¹I find then a law, that, when I would do good, evil is present with me.
> ²²For I delight in the law of God after the inward man:
> ²³But I see another law in my members, warring against the law of my mind, and bringing me into captivity to the law of sin which is in my members.
> ²⁴O wretched man that I am! who shall deliver me from the body of this death?
> ²⁵I thank God through Jesus Christ our LORD. So then with the mind I myself serve the law of God; but with the flesh the law of sin.
> ¹There is therefore now no condemnation to them which are in Christ Jesus, who walk not after the flesh, but after the Spirit. Romans 7:21-8:1

This Bitterness is no respecter of persons. He actually works in three dimensions. There is Bitterness you can have towards others, there is Bitterness you can have towards yourself, and there is Bitterness you can have towards God.

All of that is scriptural. This principality can work in all dimensions. Usually when you find Self-Bitterness, you will find it towards others because of Rejection, and usually you will find it towards God.

Forgiveness

In ministry, I always ask people to forgive God. If you have Bitterness towards God, it is time to tell Him even if He has not done anything to you because you do not understand where evil comes from. You need to forgive Him because that is your release.

The Bible says when your brother has erred against you, and you come to partake of communion and you remember your brother has erred against you, (not that you have erred against him), you leave your gift at the altar, go find your brother and make your peace with him.

Why should you do that? You have not done anything. The same thing is the reason we go and make peace with God. On the very same basis that God gives us those scriptures with one another, we go to God and ask Him to forgive us whether we did anything wrong or not. I may not have done anything wrong to you, but you may have an attitude or a problem. I am going to come to you and repent to you.

In 1993 I went back to my hometown to see my father who had brutally victimized me most of life and today we are still breached and estranged. (Henry Wright's father is deceased at the time of this printing.) I went there because God told me to go there for my soul's sake and for his.

I remember pulling up in the yard as he was washing his car. I pulled up and got out. I had not seen the man in many years.

I said, "Hi Dad."

He said, "Who are you?"

I said, "I am Henry, your son." By the way, I am an only child. "I am Henry, your son."

"I do not have a son. What did you say your name was?"

"Henry."

"Howie? Used to know a Howie one time."

This man is not senile; he is smart. That was his Bitterness, those were his devils, those were his evil spirits.

I said, "I am your son, Henry."

"I do not have a son. What is your name?"

This went on for 15 or 20 minutes. It was not a time for Rejection. As he was soaping his tires I said, "I'll hose the tires down for you if you like. You soap them, I'll hose." "What is your name again?" "I am your son, Henry."

Finally he said, "What are you doing here?" I said, "I came to ask your forgiveness. I came to repent to you, Daddy, for my Rebellion, for my Rejection as a child. I came to take responsibility for it. Can I do that today?"

Well, I finally got invited into the house. I got on my knees in that living room before my daddy, who had brutally victimized me, most of my days, physically, emotionally and verbally. I got down on my knees and I repented to him for my Rebellion and my Rejection for my soul and for his.

When I finished, his wife (my mother had died) told me privately, "He is the one that needs to be doing the repenting to you, not you to him." She said that to me afterwards.

I said, "Tina, it does not make any difference. The Word says I leave my gift at the altar and I come. My soul has to be purged of this stuff right here. What he does is between him and God. What I do is between me and God. Since I have been forgiven of 1.6 billion dollars worth of sins, the least I can do is forgive my daddy of his and take responsibility for mine before the living God."

REPENTANCE

You can come before the Lord and ask Him to deliver you from this stuff once and for all. The Word of God does not return void, but it shall accomplish that which it was sent to accomplish.

> So shall my word be that goeth forth out of my mouth: it shall not return unto me void, but it shall accomplish that which I please, and it shall prosper in the thing whereto I sent it. Isaiah 55:11

Let's set the stage for our hearts to be right as we come before God in prayer. Satan is a legalist; he is the executor of the law. We want to make sure if he is prosecuting you, the defense attorney has a chance to win this case.

The judge of all flesh, the Father, sits on the throne. Jesus Christ is your advocate; He is your intercessor; He is the One that made it possible for God to forgive you and to cleanse you.

There are those who are teaching in America today that once you become born again you never have to repent again. This is a serious doctrinal defect because it allows sin to abound and grace to abound at the same time. The Bible says it does not work that way. Do we sin more that grace may more abound? The Scripture says: God forbid.

> ¹What shall we say then? Shall we continue in sin, that grace may abound?
> ²God forbid. How shall we, that are dead to sin, live any longer therein? Romans 6:1-2

I want to read a couple of scriptures in preparation for our time of repentance. Isaiah said a humble and a contrite heart He won't deny.

> For thus saith the high and lofty One that inhabiteth eternity, whose name is Holy; I dwell in the high and holy place, with him also that is of a contrite and humble spirit, to revive the spirit of the humble, and to revive the heart of the contrite ones. Isaiah 57:15

The Book of Psalms says,

> The sacrifices of God are a broken spirit: a broken and a contrite heart, O God, thou wilt not despise. Psalm 51:17

Hebrews says,

> ⁹There remaineth therefore a rest to the people of God.
> ¹⁰For he that is entered into his rest, he also hath ceased from his own works, as God did from his.
> ¹¹Let us labour therefore to enter into that rest, lest any man fall after the same example of unbelief. Hebrews 4:9-11

The Word says when an evil spirit is cast out, he wanders through a dry place seeking a place of rest, and finding none he returns to his original home to see if the house is filled or empty. When the evil spirit is within you, when the principality of Bitterness is within you, when one of these seven spirit entities is within you, they are at rest, and you are at unrest.

When they are gone, they are in unrest and you are in rest. When you give place to them, you say to them, "Take your rest at my expense. Have a wonderful day and I'll enjoy my day of Torment and thank you for blessing me with my unrest."

Theologically, that is exactly what you are saying to them, and they say, "Thank you for inviting me." Resist the devil and he will flee. There is a place of rest for the people of God.

> For the word of God is quick, and powerful, and sharper than any twoedged sword, piercing even to the dividing asunder of soul and spirit, and of the joints and marrow, and is a discerner of the thoughts and intents of the heart.
> Hebrews 4:12

Where did Jesus say evil thoughts came from? From within, out of the heart of man.

> For from within, out of the heart of men, proceed evil thoughts, adulteries, fornications, Murders,
> Mark 7:21

As a man thinketh in his heart so is he.

> For as he thinketh in his heart, so is he: Eat and drink, saith he to thee; but his heart is not with thee.
> Proverbs 23:7

These are evil thoughts of the heart within your human spirit because they are spirit. These spirits are parasites and you are the host carrier.

> Neither is there any creature that is not manifest in his sight: but all things are naked and opened unto the eyes of him with whom we have to do.
> Hebrews 4:13

If the Word of God is quick and powerful, if it penetrates, if it exposes, if it discerns, if it tells you exactly the nature of the thoughts and intents of your heart, then the creature has to be the principalities and powers and spiritual wickedness in high places and the rulers of the darkness of this world, which is Satan, his fallen angels, and evil spirits.

These are the creatures that are manifest before His sight and they are naked. Do you think the Father and the Lord know these creatures that are invisible? Do you think they are exposed before His eyesight?

Then you need to see them as well as He sees them if you are His children. He has given you the Word, He has given you the Holy Spirit, He has given you the Lord to show you. When the Lord was here for His ministry for three and a half years, He exposed them, He showed us where they were. He showed us that they spoke through people and He cast them out with His Word.

The Lord Jesus speaking to John by his angel says,

> **Remember therefore from whence thou art fallen, and repent, and do the first works; or else I will come unto thee quickly, and will remove thy candlestick out of his place, except thou repent.** Revelation 2:5

The Lord is speaking to the church at Pergamus:

> **[13]I know thy works, and where thou dwellest, even where Satan's seat is: and thou holdest fast my name, and hast not denied my faith, even in those days wherein Antipas was my faithful martyr, who was slain among you, where Satan dwelleth.**
> **[14]But I have a few things against thee, because thou hast there them that hold the doctrine of Balaam, who taught Balac to cast a stumblingblock before the children of Israel, to**

eat things sacrificed unto idols, and to commit
fornication.

¹⁵So hast thou also them that hold the doctrine
of the Nicolaitanes, which thing I hate.

¹⁶Repent; or else I will come unto thee
quickly, and will fight against them with the
sword of my mouth.

¹⁷He that hath an ear, let him hear what the
Spirit saith unto the churches;   Revelation 2:13-17

The doctrine of Balaam is saying you can sin like
hell and God will turn the other cheek because of grace
and mercy. It is saying because you are in covenant, you
are immune to the consequences of sin.

That is a heresy. Who taught Balaam to cast a
stumbling block before the children of Israel, to eat
things sacrificed unto idols, and to commit fornication?

In the epistle of Thyatira, the Lord says,

Notwithstanding I have a few things against
thee, because thou sufferest that woman Jezebel,
which calleth herself a prophetess, to teach and
to seduce my servants to commit fornication, and
to eat things sacrificed unto idols.   Revelation 2:20

In other words there was a woman prophetess in the
church full of evil spirits and heresies and they allowed
her to stand and seemingly represent God when she
represented the devil. Jesus is saying he did not deal
with her. The church allowed her to continue when they
knew she was not of my Spirit.

²¹And I gave her space to repent of her
fornication; and she repented not.

²²Behold, I will cast her into a bed, and them
that commit adultery with her into great
tribulation, except they repent of their deeds.
Revelation 2:21-22

Revelation says,

> ²Be watchful, and strengthen the things which remain, that are ready to die: for I have not found thy works perfect before God.
> ³Remember therefore how thou hast received and heard, and hold fast, and repent. If therefore thou shalt not watch, I will come on thee as a thief, and thou shalt not know what hour I will come upon thee.   Revelation 3:2-3

Revelation says,

> ¹⁹As many as I love, I rebuke and chasten: be zealous therefore, and repent.
> ²⁰Behold, I stand at the door, and knock: if any man hear my voice, and open the door, I will come in to him, and will sup with him, and he with me.   Revelation 3:19-20

Discernment

In Nehemiah chapters 8 and 9, the children of the Jews who had gone into captivity because of sin and rebellion against God in the days of Nebuchadnezzar who were rebuilding the temple under the leadership of Nehemiah, found the law. They found the Word of God. The Word of God is discernment by my definition.

On the one hand you have your Attorney who is Jesus Christ, on the other hand you have the prosecuting attorney, who is the devil against your life, and the Judge, the Father of all flesh, is on the throne. If you repent from your heart, the judge will say you are free. Then these characters have to leave unless you meet them in the corridor outside the door or down over the hill when they come to talk to you again.

I would hang out a no vacancy sign. No room at the inn. No parasites allowed. Your choice, not my choice, not his choice, your choice. You choose what you will have this day, blessings or cursings, life or death. Your choice.

> I call heaven and earth to record this day against you, that I have set before you life and death, blessing and cursing: therefore choose life, that both thou and thy seed may live:
>
> Deuteronomy 30:19

In Nehemiah 8, when the people gathered themselves together as one man into the street, the Bible says,

> ¹And all the people gathered themselves together as one man into the street that was before the water gate; and they spake unto Ezra the scribe to bring the book of the law of Moses, which the LORD had commanded to Israel.
> ²And Ezra the priest brought the law before the congregation both of men and women, and all that could hear with understanding, upon the first day of the seventh month.
> ³And he read therein before the street that was before the water gate from the morning until midday, before the men and the women, and those that could understand; and the ears of all the people were attentive unto the book of the law. ...
> Nehemiah 8:1-3

> ⁵And Ezra opened the book in the sight of all the people; (for he was above all the people;) and when he opened it, all the people stood up:
> ⁶And Ezra blessed the LORD, the great God. And all the people answered, Amen, Amen, with lifting up their hands: and they bowed their

> heads, and worshipped the LORD with their
> faces to the ground.
>
> 7Also Jeshua, and Bani, and Sherebiah, Jamin,
> Akkub, Shabbethai, Hodijah, Maaseiah, Kelita,
> Azariah, Jozabad, Hanan, Pelaiah, and the
> Levites, caused the people to understand the law:
> and the people stood in their place.
>
> 8So they read in the book in the law of God
> distinctly, and gave the sense, and caused them to
> understand the reading.   Nehemiah 8:5-8

They were not sitting; they were standing at
attention. This lasted 12 hours. They stood, man and
woman and child, for 12 hours at attention before the
living God. They read in the book in the law of God
distinctly and He gave the sense and caused them to
understand the reading.

> 1Now in the twenty and fourth day of this
> month the children of Israel were assembled
> with fasting, and with sackclothes, and earth
> upon them.
>
> 2And the seed of Israel separated themselves
> from all strangers, and stood and confessed their
> sins, and the iniquities of their fathers.
>   Nehemiah 9:1-2

Why did they confess the iniquities of their fathers?
They read in the law of Moses in the Ten
Commandments, commandment number one concerning
idolatry. The curse of the consequences of the sin of the
fathers shall be passed on to the third and fourth
generation of them who hate God. But to them who
repent and to them who love God, it is not cursings to
three or four generations, it is blessings to thousands.

They read in the law and in the Word they were the
product of the sin of their ancestors. They desperately

needed God, and they desperately needed His provision. Why? So they would not go back into captivity on the same basis their ancestors had.

You have an option. You can go on in life or you can die in the same iniquities that have killed or are killing your ancestors.

> **Beloved, I wish above all things that thou mayest prosper and be in health, even as thy soul prospereth.** 3 John 1:2

If you have seen evidence of these iniquities causing spirits of infirmity, disease, death and insanity in your family tree, this is a chance for you to break the inherited curse. You do not have to bear those same diseases.

You do not have to live with those same diseases, and if you are not manifesting those diseases of your ancestors yet in your life, depending on your age, it can stop now. You can live to a ripe old age and never have those diseases.

The ultimate will of God for you is not to get sick and not to go into various degrees of insanity or torment. That is His perfect will.

**God's perfect will
is not to heal you,
God's perfect will is
that you do not get sick**

Humbly come before Him and deal with these issues and stay before Him all the rest of your life.

When you fall into that character when he comes around to keep that record of wrongs growing, when someone comes around you who has this stuff in them and you are exposed to them, remember what they said about Jesus: the evil one came and found nothing in Him.

> **Hereafter I will not talk much with you: for the prince of this world cometh, and hath nothing in me.**   John 14:30

You can be surrounded by evil men and it does not mean you have to be evil in return. You do not have to take Bitterness in when you are around bitter people. You do not have to get angry when you are around angry people. You do not have to go there.

When you are not walking in light because you are human and because you fell, if you would be so quick to repent, and so quick to get these characters out of your life, the curse will not have a chance to latch onto you. That is a more excellent way™.

MINISTRY

In ministry, we want to stop the forward motion of something that is wrong in your life. If it is a disease we are dealing with, we want to put the brakes on it.

In the beginning of God becoming part of your life and you becoming part of what God represents, there is a slowing down of the forward motion of what your problem represents. If you can start to see an improvement, which is a slowing down, that is the beginning of your faith to believe for the rest of it.

If this thing can be shaken, if it can be affected, then it can be defeated. Do not ever lose sight of that. The steps to producing victory are just that, steps.

The Working of Miracles

There are two dimensions of God's ability to move in your life in the area of disease. One is the realm of healing and the other is the realm of miracles. Miracles are acts of God as a work of the Holy Spirit in areas of human composition that, when affected by disease or affected by internal or external realities, cannot be healed by medical science or anything.

These are things such as nerve tissue, damaged brain cells, liver, organs, the list goes on. That would take a creative miracle in order for it to be restored.

You cannot minister healing to cirrhosis of the liver; you are wasting your time because it does not heal. You cannot minister healing to damaged nerve tissue; you are wasting your time. You cannot minister healing to damaged brain tissue from electric shock therapy; you are wasting your time. What do you have to do?

You have to ask God for a creative miracle. What is a creative miracle? It is putting back into place the very tissue that was destroyed. It cannot be healed; it has to be recreated as if it were fresh off the press.

The Gifts of Healing

Healing involves stopping the forward motion of what is causing the problem, bringing it to a grinding halt, and then reversing the direction. In the case of Hashimoto's disease or hypothyroidism, what would happen in their healing? It does not need a creative miracle.

There is nothing wrong with your thyroid; it is just either over or undersecreting thyroxin. There is a spiritual problem causing the underproduction of thyroxin. If you deal with the root problems, the malfunctioning of the thyroid comes to a grinding halt and it starts pumping out thyroxin at the proper rate.

Then your thyroid is normal. That is a healing. Something has changed upstream that allowed God to bring you back into a place of balance.

Bitterness is not a physical disease. You do not need a creative miracle to get rid of Bitterness. You do not need a healing to get rid of Bitterness. It is not a physical part of your life.

It is a spiritual part of your life. You now have your eyes wide open about what is happening invisibly within the confines of your human spirit and your human soul.

Walk Out

I have to guard my heart every single minute of the day. I have to guard my heart that I do not allow Bitterness to gain a foothold at any point. I can be totally delivered of Bitterness. I can be totally free of all seven spirits that answer to it, and it does not mean that they won't come around checking me out to see if I am filled or empty.

It does not mean they will not use other people who have these spirits in them. It does not mean I will not be subjected to defilement by people who have these spirits in them.

But because I am subjected to another person's defilement in this area does not mean I have to pick these characters back up and let them become part of my nature. It is your choice.

When this comes as temptation, you are going to feel the enemy's presence just as strongly as if you had him for thirty years. Temptation brings you the very same strength of emotion, feeling and thought as if you had the problem for a long time.

If you do not have peace of mind there are two roots, Occultism and Bitterness, who will steal your peace of mind. What is Occultism? Any modality of thought in contradiction or opposition to what the Word of God has said about the subject.

I'll tell you what Occultism looks like. "Oh, I do not believe there is a God. I just do not believe it." What does the Word of God say? The fool has said in his heart there is no God. What is the Occultism? There is no God. It is as simple as that.

You go to mathematics class and they teach you that two plus two is four, and you say, "No it is five." Which is the occultic statement? Two plus two is five is the occultic statement.

How many thumbs and fingers do I have? Ten. You know that is true. Yet Occultism can go like this. "Oh, I have eleven: ten, nine, eight, seven, six (counting down the fingers on one hand), and five (holding up the other hand) is 11. Which is the occultic statement? I took truth, I took a physical reality and I manipulated it to offer another statement which was error. However, are six plus five equal to eleven?

Say you are a runner and you just ran the 440 and then you lay it down. Next year it comes time to run and you have been out here eating barbeque and other things, and your coach comes and says, "I need to have you run the 440 tomorrow."

"That is great. I won that thing last year. I'll be right there at 7:00." You are there at 7:00. You get up on that old starting block and you take off. Guess who's going to win the 440? It will not be you.

You may have it in your heart to win that 440, but if you have not continually applied the conditioning principles to make you victorious, then you are kidding yourself.

Walking the spiritual walk
requires daily practice

When you run the race, you keep in shape. Paul said in the New Testament the only way you can win a race is to stay in it. It is not who starts the race; it is who finishes it.

You say, "This is too much work. I just do not want to apply myself to spiritual things. I had just as soon go back to my old ways. You are asking me to do stuff that requires energy and effort, and I have to think, and I have to read my Bible at least once every six months, and I have to pray to God at least twice a year, that is just too much."

I made a statement to myself many years ago. When those thoughts came to me I said this, "I would rather be weary from defeating my enemy than worn out and wasted from losing to him."

The Word says the spirit of man shall sustain him in his infirmity. Have you ever seen anyone just give up the will to live? What is the difference between that person and the person who is living?

There is a spiritual problem that comes, the spirit of Death and the spirit of Hopelessness. A person can die when there is no organic reason. They do not have a disease, they just die on the inside. That is not finishing the race. The human spirit belongs to God. In fact the Word says this, the spirit of man is a candle of the Lord.

The spirit of man is the candle of the LORD,
searching all the inward parts of the belly.
Proverbs 20:27

TYPES OF BITTERNESS

The types of Bitterness we have dealt with are:

- Bitterness against others
- Bitterness against yourself
- Bitterness against God

Three dimensions of spiritual bondage are Bitterness against others, against yourself, and against God. You have to guard your heart.

Jacob and Esau

You know the story of Jacob and Rebecca his mother, and how they connived to deceive Isaac of Esau's birthright. When Jacob was running for his life from Esau after stealing from him the inheritance, he stopped to build an altar unto the Lord at Bethel.

Years later he is on the way back to meet Esau and he is really courageous. He puts all the servants up front, all of his wives up front, all the cows, donkeys and billy goats up front, and he is the last one.

If any one of them is going to get killed, he is the last one. He is a really courageous individual. He stops at Bethel and builds an altar where God met him the first time and delivered him from Esau. He stops and he sacrifices unto the Lord and he remembers the first victory and he trusts God will sustain him in the second victory.

He goes back to the first place of sacrifice before God, the first place where he laid his heart down before

God and God met him. He does it again in his Fear. Not in his faith, but in his Fear he submits to God. He makes his peace, starts his journey, and here comes his brother.

Esau ran to him, embraced him, kissed him on the cheek and forgave him everything. Esau had a right to have Bitterness. The real tragedy about this story is that Esau is the unrenewed and unregenerated one. Jacob represents the renewed, masterful, victorious son of God.

Esau was more spiritual. He forgave and released Jacob. He loved him and blessed him. He said, "Come on, I'll share my land with you. Are you coming back brother? Hey, I have lots of land you can have. Bring Rebecca and the kids, come on and let's get together and have a good time and you can have your portion of land and I'll take mine. No hard feelings."

You are going to have an opportunity to meet these characters every single day. What you do with them is up to you. If God has broken the power of these things over your life and you are walking in your freedom, then keep walking. Keep walking, do not let anything steal your joy and steal your peace. It is not worth it.

RULING PRINCIPALITIES

How do I know they are principalities? I know they are principalities because they rule people in a rulership position. There are other spiritual dynamics that are not greater than them, but feed them and are subordinate to them, and you see them by their fruit.

In other words, if you saw Resentment, Resentment is not greater than this. If you are watching these things manifest all over the place, you may see Violence, but what is behind Violence? Violence is not the principality; it is the fruit of the principality.

Murder is not a principality; it is the fruit of the principality. Hatred is not a principality; it is subordinate to Bitterness.

In other words, these become obvious because this is the predominate figurehead for that area of breakdown in human nature. Bitterness does not come from Hatred. Bitterness does not come from Anger. Bitterness does not come from Murder. It is a ruling principality because it shows up and there is nothing above it any greater in that area.

Plus the scripture in Hebrews 12:15 does not say looking diligently lest a root of Resentment springing up trouble you. It does not say lest a root of Retaliation springing up trouble you. It says looking diligently lest a root of Bitterness springing up trouble you. Bitterness.

Double Minded Peter

Jesus said to that great man Peter who was a foundation of the church, "Satan desires to sift you like wheat and when you have recovered yourself, strengthen the brethren." Jesus was saying: "Mr. Great Disciple, Mr. Great Apostle, you have a problem."

Jesus was talking about dying for you and me and going to the cross, and Peter puffed up and said, "No way, Jose, You are not going to do that, Lord." The Lord turned around and said, "Get behind me, Satan."

Peter did not leave the ministry. He got the point. Peter had an evil spirit and it manifested. When that thing manifested, he went into Fear. He went into denial. He denied Christ, and then he got it straight. When he recovered himself from the snare of the devil, he was able to strengthen the brethren.

Peter did not have it all together. He still had an evil spirit. He still had Fear of Man. Paul met him one day and saw that Peter, when he was with the Jews would act like the circumcision. When he was with the Gentiles he would act like a Gentile, because he got the revelation they were clean.

He was double minded. He was a hypocrite. He would get over here with the Jewish boys and say, "Yeah those Gentile Christians, you know they are just a bunch of goof balls." He would get over here with the Gentile Christians, and say, "You guys are the righteous through Christ Jesus. I sure love you."

Paul observed this double mindedness and came up to him one day and said, "Peter, you are a hypocrite." He rebuked him openly and said, "You have a spiritual problem, man. When you are with the Jews, you act like the Jews and when you are with the Gentiles you act like the Gentiles. Have you not heard there is neither Jew nor Gentile in Christ anymore? What is your problem?"

Peter got it straightened out one more time. Do you know what I like about Peter? He might have been a hothead, he might have had Fear of Man, he may have had spiritual problems, but he was teachable and repentant.

The ingredients for being in ministry are that you do not have to be perfect. You do not have to be learned; you only have to be teachable and repentant. We are to be blessings to each other, not cursings. The free flowing back and forth is so very important.

Appendix

INTERACTION OF STRONG MEN

If you are still struggling with Bitterness and Resentment and you do not feel like you are free, it is because Rejection is fueling it. Rejection can be an open door for Bitterness. You just have someone reject you and that high-octane ping goes off on the inside.

You cannot understand how to deal with Rejection if you do not deal with Bitterness. Rejection fuels Bitterness. If I dealt with Rejection it would not go because Bitterness would be there fueling it.

First you have to get Bitterness defined and shown up, because without that you will not be able to deal with the Rejection. It is impossible to deal with Rejection unless you have Bitterness dealt with.

How are you going to deal with Rejection if you cannot forgive? How are you going to deal with Rejection if you still have Resentment and Anger and Hatred and Violence and Murder? We have Bitterness and Rejection running side by side.

Rebellion is right beside it. We will deal with Witchcraft after Rejection. We will deal with Witchcraft because Witchcraft comes along and takes the Bitterness and takes the Rejection. Witchcraft is fueled by something else called Fear.

We have four principalities. We have Bitterness, Rejection, Fear, and Witchcraft. Witchcraft is not a principality. Occultism is the principality. Witchcraft is the spirit that answers to it.

Occultism in the Word is an antichrist spirit. An antichrist spirit represents everything against the Word.

> **For rebellion is as the sin of witchcraft, and stubbornness is as iniquity and idolatry. Because thou hast rejected the word of the LORD, he hath also rejected thee from being king.** 1 Samuel 15:23

Stubbornness is self-idolatry. You are god.

"Bless God, you are not going to make me do anything I do not want to do."

"I'll see you in chapel at 8:00."

"Yeah, if I feel like it I'll be there."

Bless God, nothing is going to happen unless you feel like it.

Rebellion is as the sin of witchcraft. In the study of Saul, he listened to the voice of the people and not to God. That is why it is an antichrist spirit because anything that will not obey the Word of God is anti-Word.

If the Word says you must forgive your brother and you are not going to, that is an anti-Word thought. If it is an anti-Word thought, it is an antichrist thought because the Word came and became flesh as Jesus, the Christ.

Witchcraft is fueled by Fear. Witchcraft is like Rebellion; so you have Fear. There is a lot of overlap when it comes to the interaction of these principalities. Rejection fuels Bitterness. Bitterness is fueled also by Rejection, but they are separate.

Fear is not one with Rebellion. It is not one with Witchcraft. Rebellion and Witchcraft are one and the same.

Fear is another principality that lines up with those to reinforce them. Witchcraft takes additional power from the principality of Fear. They are working together, but they are separate.

They can be independent, but they are more powerful when they are together. Bitterness and Rejection can work independently, but they are more powerful when they are entwined together. It is a greater bondage.

Yet, Jesus' work on the cross overcame all.